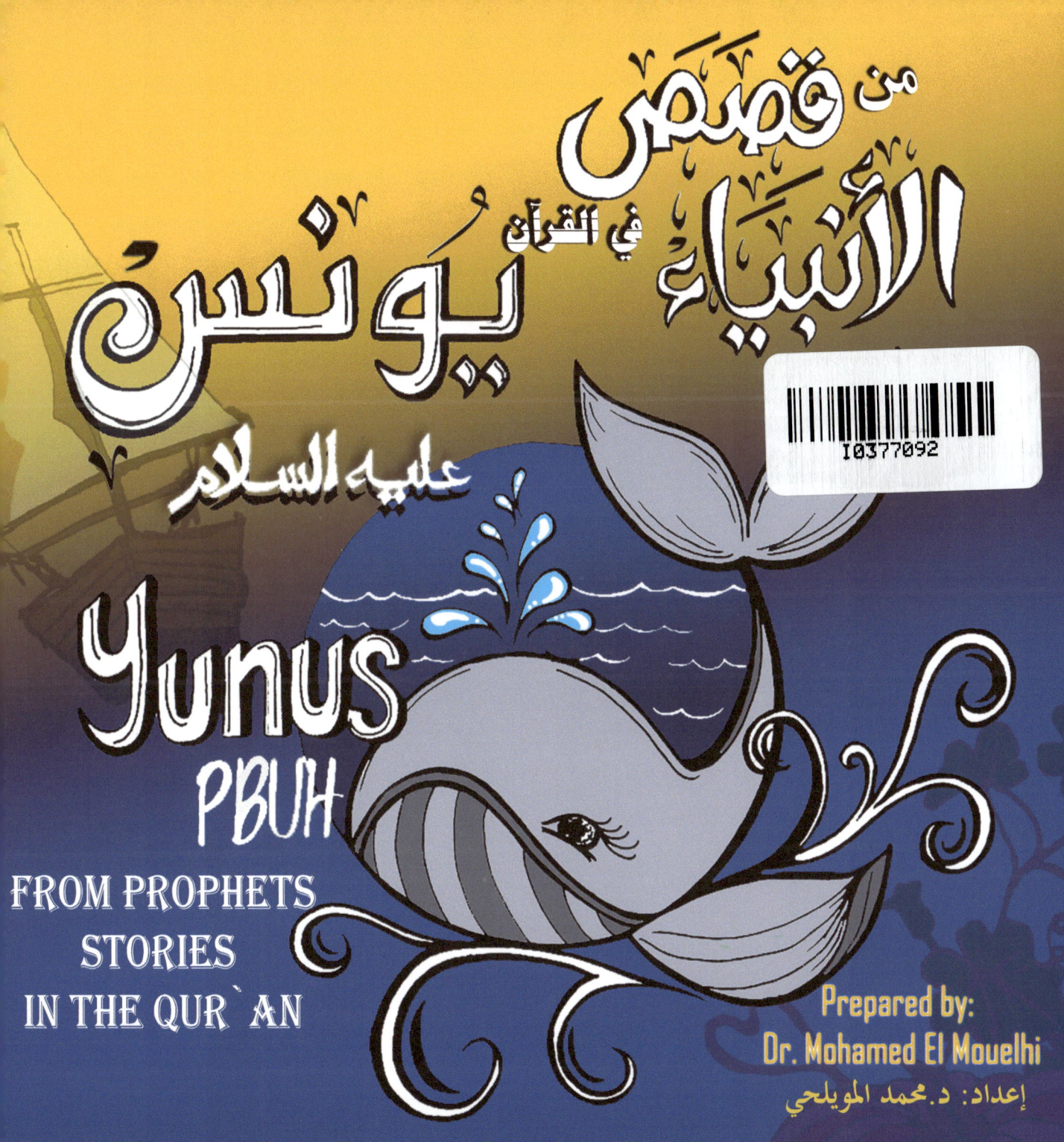

Text Copyright © 2021 by Mohamed El Mouelhi.

Illustrations Copyright © 2021 by Hossam El Mouelhi and Donia Farouk.

All Rights Reserved. No part of this book may be reproduced, transmitted, or stored in an information retrieval system in any form or by any means, graphic, electronic, or mechanical, including photocopying, taping, and recording, without prior written permission from the publisher.

جميع الحقوق محفوظة.

ISBN 978-1-7357701-2-3

First edition 2021

Published by Honey Elm Books LLC
www.HoneyElmBooks.com

Yunus (Jonah) PBUH

يونس عليه السلام

Editing: Noha Elmouelhi

Artistic Preparation: Hossam El Mouelhi - Donia Farouk

تحرير: نهى المويلحي

الإعداد الفني: حسام المويلحي- دنيا فاروق

A long time ago, there was a tribe who lived in an area in what is now northern Iraq.
They lived in prosperity - an easy life full of many blessings.

فى قديم الزمان كان هناك قوم يعيشون فى شمال العراق وقد كانوا يعيشون فى رخاء ويسر ..

But they did not give thanks to Allah and worshipped other gods instead. Allah sent them Yunus to advise them to worship only Allah. His people didn't believe him... and continued to associate others with Allah. They made fun of Yunus when he warned them of Allah's coming punishment.

ولكنهم لم يشكروا الله وعبدوا آلهة أخرى، وأرسل الله سيدنا يونس (عليه السلام) لدعوة قومه إلى عبادة الله وحده، ولكنهم رفضوا رسالته واستمروا في شركهم بالله، واستهزأوا به عندما أنذرهم بحلول عذاب الله.

They mocked him when Allah's torment
didn't happen immediately.
Yunus was offended and lost patience with them.
He abandoned his people without the permission
of Allah. Yunus left in anger, and thought
that Allah would not punish him.

أزدادت سخريتهم عندما لم ينزل بهم عذاب الله الذي هددهم به.

ولم يصبر يونس (عليه السلام) على تكذيب قومه له وسخريتهم منه، فتركهم دون إذن من الله، وذهب غاضباً منهم وظن أن الله لن يحاسبه على ذلك.

"So wait with patience for the Decision of your Lord, and be not like the Companion of the Fish - when he cried out (to Us) while he was in deep sorrow".

(Al-Qalam: 48)

سُورَةُ القَلَمِ

بِسْمِ اللَّهِ الرَّحْمَٰنِ الرَّحِيمِ

فَاصْبِرْ لِحُكْمِ رَبِّكَ وَلَا تَكُن كَصَاحِبِ الْحُوتِ إِذْ نَادَىٰ وَهُوَ مَكْظُومٌ ﴿٤٨﴾

He ran away to the coast, angry
with his people.
Yunus found a ship that was ready to sail,
and boarded it.
However, the ship was too full and was
in danger of sinking in the middle of the sea.

وفر منهم إلى الشاطئ وهو غاضب منهم، ووجد سفينة على وشك الإقلاع فركب بها.
كانت السفينة عليها حمولة كبيرة تزيد عن تحملها وكادت أن تغرق في منتصف البحر.

The ship's crew suggested that they cast lots to choose someone to get off the ship to lessen the weight. Yunus agreed to participate in the casting of lots along with all other passengers. His name was picked three times in a row, and so Yunus was thrown overboard.

إقترح طاقم السفينة القيام بقرعة بين الركاب لإختيار من يلقونه خارج السفينة لتقليل حمولتها. فإشترك يونس (عليه السلام) مع باقي الركاب في القرعة فكان الإسم الذي أقترعوه ثلاث مرات متتالية هو يونس.... وكان إسمه هو الخاسر، وبناءً عليه تم إلقاؤه خارج السفينة.

"When he ran to the laden ship,
Then he (agreed to) cast lots,
and he was among the losers"
(Al-Safat: 140–141)

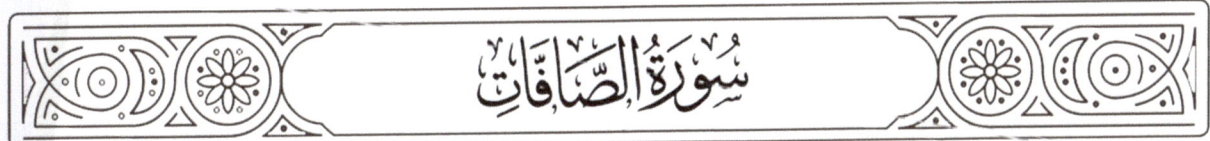

إِذْ أَبَقَ إِلَى ٱلْفُلْكِ ٱلْمَشْحُونِ ۝ فَسَاهَمَ فَكَانَ مِنَ ٱلْمُدْحَضِينَ ۝

Yunus was thrown into the water
where he wrestled the waves trying to stay alive.

Then, a big fish (a whale) came and swallowed him.

Yunus realized that he had done something wrong.

سقط يونس (عليه السلام) في الماء، وأخذ يصارع الأمواج ثم جاء حوت كبير وأبتلعه، حينها أدرك أنه إرتكب خطأ ما.

Yunus had gone through many challenges, starting with his people denying his message. He had gotten fed up with their continued refusal of his call to worship only Allah. He had decided to abandon them and left without Allah's permission.

لقد مر يونس بمصاعب عديدة، وكانت أول المصاعب أن قومه لم يؤمنوا به وكذبوه، وحينها لم يصبر على قومه لإستمرارهم في رفض دعوته للإيمان بالله وحده، فتركهم دون أن يأذن الله له.

As a result,

his situation got worse and worse.

The ship he ran away in was going to sink.

Then, when they cast lots, his name had come up

three times to get thrown overboard.

نتيجة لذلك إزدادت حالته سوءاً. فعندما كان على السفينة وكادت أن تغرق، وإختياره لإلقائه في البحر بعد إقتراع إسمه ثلاث مرات متتالية.

And finally, while in the sea,
he was swallowed by a whale.
And now, he was inside this big whale, in the dark,
in the middle of nowhere.

وأخيراً يبتلعه الحوت، وهو الآن في بطن الحوت في الظلام
في مكان مجهول في البحر.

"Then a whale swallowed him as he had done an act worthy of blame".
(Al-Safat:142)

فَالْتَقَمَهُ الْحُوتُ وَهُوَ مُلِيمٌ ﴿١٤٢﴾

Yunus had strong faith in Allah and was always grateful for His Blessings. Had he not been among those who glorify Allah, he would have remained inside the whale until the Day of Judgement. But he turned to Allah to save him and said this prayer:

وكان يونس قوي الإيمان ومن الذين يسبحون الله ويحمدونه على نعمه، ولولا ذلك لبقى في بطن الحوت إلى يوم القيامة ولكن يونس دعا ربه لينجيه وقال :

"None has the right to be worshipped but You Allah, Glorified and Exalted are You. Truly, I have been of the wrong-doers."
(Sura Al-Anbiya: 87):

سُورَةُ الأَنْبِيَاءِ

بِسْمِ اللَّهِ الرَّحْمَٰنِ الرَّحِيمِ

.... لَّا إِلَٰهَ إِلَّا أَنتَ سُبْحَانَكَ إِنِّي

كُنتُ مِنَ الظَّالِمِينَ ۟

So, Allah answered his prayer,
as Yunus had often remembered Allah
and he had full trust in Him.
Almighty Allah saved Yunus, and orderd
the whale to spit Yunus out onto the shore.
Yunus was fatigued and sick after
being inside the whale.

فأستجاب له ربه لان يونس كان كثير الذكر وكان إيمانه بالله قوي وثقته بالله لا حدود لها، فنجاه الله من أزمته وأمر الله الحوت أن يلفظه علي أرض يابسة وهو في حالة ضعف ومرض من بقائه داخل بطن الحوت.

Out of Allah's Mercy,

Allah grew a pumpkin tree over Yunus to shade him with its large leaves and to protect him from the intense light and heat of the sun.

ومن رحمة الله له أنه أنبت شجرة من القرع ذات الأوراق الكبيرة فوقه لتقيه من حرارة الجو وضوء الشمس.

"Had he not been among those who glorify Allah, he would have indeed remained inside its belly (the fish) till the Day of Resurrection. But We cast him forth on the naked shore while he was sick, And We caused a tree of pumpkin to grow over him".

(Al-Safat: 143-146)

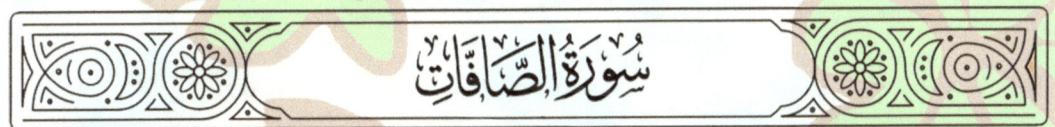

بِسْمِ اللَّهِ الرَّحْمَٰنِ الرَّحِيمِ

فَلَوْلَا أَنَّهُ كَانَ مِنَ الْمُسَبِّحِينَ ﴿١٤٣﴾ لَلَبِثَ فِي بَطْنِهِ إِلَىٰ يَوْمِ يُبْعَثُونَ ﴿١٤٤﴾ فَنَبَذْنَاهُ بِالْعَرَاءِ وَهُوَ سَقِيمٌ ﴿١٤٥﴾ وَأَنبَتْنَا عَلَيْهِ شَجَرَةً مِّن يَقْطِينٍ ﴿١٤٦﴾

Yunus spent some time under
the shade of the pumpkin tree
until he regained his health and strength.
During Yunus` absence, his people realized
the wrong of their ways.
They asked Allah to forgive them and repented
to Him before it is too late.

ولبث يونس لفترة من الزمن فى العراء تحت ظل أوراق شجرة القرع حتى أسترد صحته وقوته، وفى غياب سيدنا يونس عن قومه أدركوا خطأهم بتكذيبهم له وأستغفروا الله على ذنوبهم وآمنوا بالله وندموا على معصيتهم قبل فوات الآوان.

Because of regret of their disobedience to Prophet Yunus and their repentance before the predetermined punishment would have been inflicted on them, Allah forgave them. Allah blessed them with a prosperous life.

فغفر الله لهم ذنوبهم وتكذيبهم لنبيهم يونس قبل أن يحل عليهم عذاب الله الذى حذرهم منه نبيهم، وأنعم الله عليهم بمعيشة فى رخاء .

"And We sent him to a hundred thousand (people) or even more. And they believed; so We gave them enjoyment for a while."

(Al-Safat:147-148)

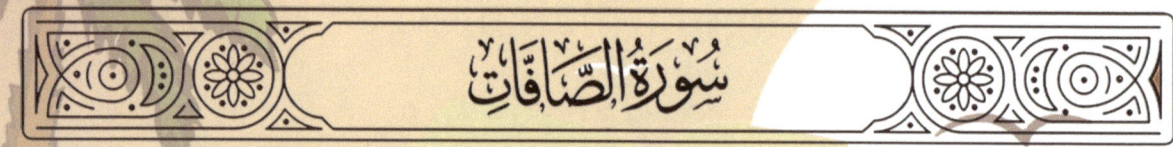

بِسْمِ اللَّهِ الرَّحْمَٰنِ الرَّحِيمِ

وَأَرْسَلْنَٰهُ إِلَىٰ مِا۟ئَةِ أَلْفٍ أَوْ يَزِيدُونَ ۝ فَـَٔامَنُوا۟ فَمَتَّعْنَٰهُمْ إِلَىٰ حِينٍ ۝

We learn from this story
to always remember Allah,
especially when we are facing
challenging times.
We must be patient and have faith
that Allah will answer our prayers.

نتعلم من هذه القصة أن نذكر الله دائما، ونزيد من ذكره عند مواجهة المصاعب، ويجب علينا أن نصبر وأن نثق أن الله سيجيب دعاءنا.

Watch a special reading of Yunus PBUH by the author!

Scan this QR code to access the video.

www.ingramcontent.com/pod-product-compliance
Lightning Source LLC
Chambersburg PA
CBHW042256100526
44589CB00002B/39